ROMAN ROADS
IN BRITAIN

Hugh Davies

Series Editor: James Dyer

SHIRE
ARCHAEOLOGY

First published in Great Britain in 2008 by Shire
Publications, part of Bloomsbury Publishing Plc
PO Box 883, Oxford, OX1 9PL, UK
1385 Broadway, 5th Floor, New York, NY 10018, USA
Email: shire@shirebooks.co.uk
www.shirebooks.co.uk

First published 2008; reprinted 2010, 2011, 2012,
2013, 2016, 2017 and 2018.

A CIP catalogue record for this book is available from
the British Library.

Shire Archaeology no. 90
ISBN 13: 978 0 74780 690 5

Designed by Ken Vail Graphic Design, Cambridge,
UK and typeset in Perpetua and Bembo.
Printed in China through World Print Ltd.

18 19 20 21   15 14 13 12 11 10 9 8

COVER IMAGE
Ackling Dyke, Wiltshire, looking north-east
towards Old Sarum (see page 34).
© Hugh Davies.

ACKNOWLEDGEMENTS
All uncredited photographs and illustrations are
by the author, and are covered by his copyright.

I would like to thank the following individuals for
their assistance on specific topics: Paul Bidwell
(Roman bridge at Corbridge); Jonathan Butler
(English Heritage Photo Library); Rose Desmond
and Anne Betts (Aerial Photography Library at the
Unit for Landscape Modelling, Cambridge
University); John Howard (Roman culverts); Adrian
James, Library of the Society of Antiquaries (Roman
Monument at Richborough); John Porter (date of
Stanegate); David Woolliscroft, Gask Ridge Project,
University of Liverpool (Innerpeffray Roman
cutting); and staff at the Royal Commission on the
Ancient and Historical Monuments of Scotland
(RCAHMS).

I would like to thank James Dyer for offering me the
opportunity to write this book, and Russell Butcher,
Sarah Hodder and Nick Wright at Shire Publications
for their help and encouragement throughout.

I owe a particular debt of gratitude to my wife Gillian
for her help and support during the project, ranging
from accompanying me on site visits to proofreading
drafts of the manuscript.

Shire Publications is supporting the Woodland Trust, the UK's leading woodland conservation charity, by funding the dedication of trees.

CONTENTS

LIST OF ILLUSTRATIONS

1

INTRODUCTION

THE Roman army began its invasion of Britain in the late summer of AD 43, heralding the end of the Iron Age and the start of a period, nearly four centuries long, in which Britain was part of the Roman Empire. Almost as soon as they arrived the Roman army began building a network of roads that rivals, in length and solidity, Britain's modern motorway and trunk road system. This book describes what we know of the Roman road network in Britain, how and why it was built, and the way its influence can still be traced in the modern landscape (figures 1 and 2).

The roads were needed initially to support the military occupation, allowing troops, equipment and supplies to be moved efficiently. But there soon arose a need for civilian travel as well, to and from newly created Roman towns. Urban life was something quite new to Iron Age Britain, but was an essential element of being part of the Roman Empire.

Yet finding out precisely how and why the roads were built is not as straightforward as might be expected. Very little written material about road-building has survived from the Roman era; in particular there are no engineering manuals or training instructions for road-builders. It is sometimes suggested that the Roman architect Vitruvius provided a method of construction based on four layers, but, as we shall see in chapter 3 he was probably discussing the courtyard of a building. Another writer, Statius, describes watching a road gang at work in southern Italy; while he probably provides an accurate description, he was a poet, not an engineer, and does not claim to be giving advice on how the job should be done. Also missing is any specific reference to planning a road alignment; the Romans are famous for the straightness of their roads, which requires skilled surveying over long distances. By contrast, substantial evidence survives about Roman land surveying, enabling us to make deductions about how these techniques could have been used by road designers.

Once roads have been built, plans are needed to show where they are; by good fortune, two fine examples have survived. The first, known as the Peutinger Table,

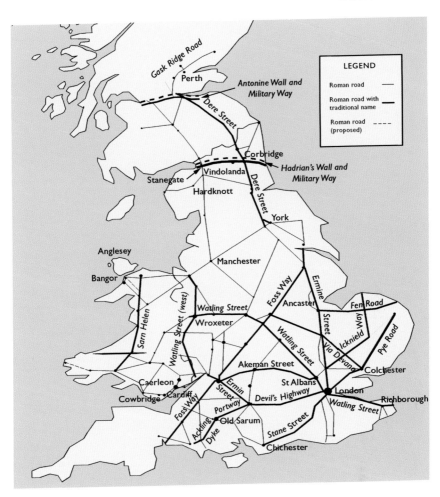

1. Diagram of major Roman roads, highlighting those with traditional names.

is a Roman road atlas covering the entire Empire; it is drawn on a long length of parchment that can be wrapped on a rod and carried conveniently by travellers. To fit the map onto such a long, thin format, the north–south scale has been compressed, relative to the east–west scale. Even so, the map would certainly have been useful for long-distance travellers: besides roads, it shows towns, mountain ranges, rivers and a tunnel. Unfortunately the part covering Britain, being at the outer end of the parchment, has all but disappeared, so cannot be used as a means of confirming what the main parts of the British road network were like when the map was prepared, probably in the second century. Another second-century

7

2. *The Devil's Highway, heading west across Crowthorne Woods, south of Bracknell, Berkshire (SU 648879). The track is a preserved right-of-way, but the trees alongside obscure the Roman ditches, and would not have been allowed to grow close to the road in Roman times.*

document, the Antonine Itinerary, is, as its name implies, a list of places along a series of routes. It too covers the whole Empire, but in this case the British section is undamaged. This contains fifteen lists of places, with distances between, seeming to suggest a series of journeys. Some stretches of road are included several times in different journeys, while others, which we know existed, such as Stane Street, do not appear at all. The document has been of great value in identifying the correct Latin name for various places – something that has often proved difficult – but is of limited value in locating most of the road network. The only other item relevant directly to British Roman roads is a fleeting reference to roads being poor in winter, made in the copy of a letter found near Hadrian's Wall, part of the famous collection of Vindolanda Tablets.

Because of this dearth of contemporary documents, most of what we have discovered has come from archaeological investigation. Fortunately, as we shall see in this book, there is a wealth of this information, which, when combined with an understanding of modern road-building and a wider historical perspective on the Roman invasion, enables us to build up a reasonably good picture of what the Roman road network was like and how it was used.

In the next chapter we examine the extent of the Roman network, and how it developed over time: first in following the Roman legions as they spread out across the country; and later as it became the essential support for civilian life in the towns that soon began to develop. As mentioned above, chapter 3 shows how the famous straight alignments were achieved, along with the characteristic Roman style of road-building. Chapter 4 shows how the famous names, such as Watling Street and Foss Way, came about after the Romans had left Britain's shores (see also Appendix 3). Since not all Roman roads have names, this chapter also describes a modern and more comprehensive method of identification, in the form of a numbering system. Chapter 5 describes what happened to the roads themselves in later centuries, while chapter 6 shows how these roads continue to influence the landscape. Finally we look at how to find out more, both for general interest and as an aid to exploring the network for oneself. After a concluding chapter, there is a list of museums to visit; these are useful sources of local information about the Roman network.

There are three appendices: the first defines some Latin terms that are used throughout the book; the second is a list of modern place names with their Roman equivalents. Some Roman sites, such as *Verulamium*, were abandoned after the Roman period; in such cases the nearest post-Roman settlement is used, in this case St Albans. The only exception in the book is *Vindolanda*, the name of a Roman fort near Hadrian's Wall, which is more commonly used than its modern name of Chesterholm. The third is a list of Roman roads, identified by their traditional names and showing where they start and finish.

Throughout the book, reference is frequently made to countries – England, Wales, Scotland – or counties within Britain; this is convenient as a means of identifying an area, but it should be remembered that all of these names post-date the Roman era. During the occupation, the island of *Britannia* was usually considered as a province, with subdivisions based on the Iron Age tribal areas. The boundaries of these subdivisions do not relate to either the modern Welsh or Scottish borders with England.

2

THE EXTENT OF THE
ROMAN ROAD NETWORK

THE roads shown in figure 1 (page 7) are the result of a long period of development, both in extent, as the roads spread across the country, and in purpose, as military requirements gave way to civilian ones. Note that, in the figure, those roads with traditional names are highlighted in bold for ease of identification. This does not indicate their importance during the Roman period: as we shall see in chapter 4, these names were established long after the end of the Roman occupation.

The history of Roman roads is intimately connected with the history of the Roman occupation itself; initially of course this meant military road-building. It is important to emphasise that the army did not build roads ahead of its campaigning front; to move around in unoccupied territory the troops would have used existing tracks and open ground. But soon after occupying an area, surveyors and engineers would have begun to construct roads that could be used to supply the front line, and link any fortified positions that the army constructed. To begin with, these would have been quite crude affairs by Roman standards, probably a strip of cleared ground with drainage ditches and perhaps some metalling. Only later would work have begun on a permanent structure. The rest of this chapter looks at how the road network followed the course of the invasion across Britain; methods of surveying and construction are covered in chapter 3.

HOW THE LEGIONS CONQUERED BRITAIN

In AD 43 the Roman army landed in Kent (perhaps also in Sussex) with a force of forty thousand men, comprising four legions of five thousand men each, and an equal number of auxiliary troops to support them. These legions were Legio II Augusta (from Upper Germany), Legio IX Hispana (originally from Spain), Legio XIV (from Upper Germany) and Legio XX Valeria (from Lower Germany). After the initial engagement to capture Colchester, the tribal centre of the hostile Catuvellauni tribe, the legions split up, apparently taking responsibility for particular regions. Legio II, under Vespasian, a future emperor, headed south and west; Legio

XIV went towards the Midlands and north Wales; Legio IX was allocated to East Anglia; and Legio XX consolidated the base at Colchester, building the first legionary fortress there. Though it is not possible to pin down precisely where units were stationed at any particular time, by the end of the first few decades of occupation, Legio II had built a fortress at Exeter, Legio XIV was based at Wroxeter, Legio IX at Lincoln, while Legio XX had abandoned the fortress at Colchester and set up at Gloucester. Around AD 80, Legio XIV was withdrawn from Britain, to be replaced at Wroxeter by Legio XX. Legio IX moved to a permanent base at York and Legio II to another at Caerleon. The final change of location took Legio XX from Wroxeter to Chester, but not before a short-lived move to a fortress at Inchtuthil near Perth in Scotland. Besides these large bases there were hundreds of forts, fortlets, signal stations and temporary camps, which were occupied from time to time, including of course those on the major frontier installations on Hadrian's Wall and the Antonine Wall. All of these required roads to allow movement of troops and supplies to provision and occupy them. The role played by some of these roads is described below.

WATLING STREET SOUTH OF THE THAMES: GATEWAY TO BRITAIN

The Roman army began its invasion and occupation of Britain with a landing on the east coast of Kent at Richborough. The spot was chosen to allow the fleet of several hundred ships to be beached and to provide a site for a defendable beachhead while the force established itself on land. Though many of the British tribes were friendly, the Romans anticipated opposition from others, in particular the Catuvellauni, who were based at Colchester. Thus the first strategic objective was to reach and occupy this centre, which meant moving up to the Thames, establishing a crossing, and then turning north-east to attack *Camulodunum*, the name given by the Romans to Colchester. The road that the Romans built to reach the Thames is now known as Watling Street. To begin with it would have been a fairly basic affair designed to support the invading troops, perhaps just a strip of cleared ground with shallow drainage ditches alongside a lightly metalled track. It soon grew to become an important civilian route into Britain, marked at its beginning by a massive Monument, visible to visitors approaching from the sea (figures 3, 4 and 5). The fort at Richborough was replaced by a small town, and even after the growth of other ports of entry such as London and Chichester, Richborough retained its status as the symbolic entrance to Britain. Eventually the Monument was demolished and an outer perimeter of defences was established to enable Richborough to join other forts along the coast in defence against Saxon invasions.

The road reached the Thames at a point very near to present-day London Bridge; this was, and still is, a convenient location for a bridge because of the existence of a

3. Richborough Castle, the Roman fort of Rutupiae, Kent (TR 328606), looking west along the line of Watling Street. Visitors to Roman Britain began their journey along this road, after passing through the Great Monument, the foundations of which can be seen in the foreground. The walls are those of the late Roman defences against the Saxons, erected long after the monument had been demolished. Though the start of Watling Street is clear, its course on the way to Canterbury is still uncertain.

4. The Roman fort at Richborough, Kent (TR 318610). Watling Street can be seen starting at the Great Monument (the foundations of which are at the left (eastern) end of the picture), before heading west out of the fort at the start of its route to London and the north-west. (Copyright reserved Cambridge University Collection of Air Photographs)

THE GREAT MONUMENT AT RICHBOROUGH

5. A reconstruction of the front elevation of the Great Monument at Richborough, Kent, not showing the likely addition of decoration and statuary. The structure, over 26 metres high, was clearly visible to visitors as they approached the port, and represented the practical and symbolic entry to Britain. Watling Street began from the far side of the monument, to take travellers to Canterbury, London and the Thames crossing. (Drawing © Society of Antiquaries of London)

gravel spur, and was where the Romans located the first Thames crossing. There was no significant settlement at all where London is now, but a settlement soon appeared, and grew to become the largest town in Roman Britain. Its success was due to the bridge itself and to the opportunities for river-borne trade on the Thames.

THE GREAT ROAD: ACCESS TO COLCHESTER

The Great Road is the name given to the link between the Thames crossing and Colchester. Following the successful storming of the tribal base there, the Romans set up a legionary fortress on the site, built a temple to Emperor Claudius, and later established the first *colonia*, a town largely established for retired soldiers (figure 6). There would have been a great deal of traffic between Colchester and the Thames crossing, necessitating substantial road construction and maintenance. Evidence of this has been shown in excavations, especially at Old Ford, where the road crosses the River Lea.

ROADS FROM COLCHESTER: THE LEGIONS SPREAD OUT ACROSS BRITAIN

Though its first role was in support of the early campaign to capture and hold Colchester, the Great Road soon joined others, such as *via Devana* and Pye Road (heading for tribal bases at Leicester and Caistor, respectively) in providing links to the legions as they fanned out from their first base. The Great Road was the first of a number of routes to the west, such as Devil's Highway, Portway and Ackling Dyke, and it linked, via the tribal capital at Silchester, through to another at Dorchester and the early fortress at Exeter. Silchester seems to have become a major transport hub in its own right, with routes to Chichester, Bath, Cirencester and across the River Severn into south Wales.

6. The partially rebuilt remains of the Balkerne Gate (TM 020257), a monumental double arch that marked the entry into Roman Colchester (Colonia Victricensis) from Londinium and Verulamium, along some of the earliest roads in Roman Britain. The monument survived Boudicca's destruction of the city in AD 61, and was later incorporated into the newly erected town wall.

WATLING STREET NORTH OF THE THAMES

The Great Road also gave access to the section of Watling Street north of the Thames, which passed through St Albans and Wroxeter, and continued into north Wales and Anglesey. It is possible that the section beyond Leicester was originally an extension of *via Devana*. (Though the main route does not pass through the town, it is known that a link road leaves the west gate and joins Watling Street further on.) This would

7. Portway, between Silchester and Old Sarum (SU 530480), north-east of Andover, Hampshire.

have provided Legio XIV with a link from Colchester to their campaigning area in the English Midlands and north Wales. Soon, however, an important link was made from the Devil's Highway, west of London (modern Marble Arch), to carry Watling Street through St Albans to connect London to the north-west and Wales. A direct link between the Thames Bridge and the section of Watling Street north of the Thames has not been established: visitors from Kent, or indeed those landing at the port, would first have been taken north to the forum and basilica; from here they would have turned west, before reaching Watling Street. It is just possible that there was originally such a link, when Roman London comprised a few roadside traders near the bridge, but perhaps it was later obscured by the main street grid of the Roman town.

STANE STREET

This road linked the southern end of the Thames crossing with Chichester, on the south coast of England. Near Chichester is the site of the huge palace of Fishbourne, but before that was built, there was a military port and supply base there, roughly contemporary with the landing base at Richborough in Kent. Stane Street was an important link in the early road network, and passes close to the large villa at Bignor, West Sussex. The fact that, at the northern end, the alignment points directly at Chichester has given rise to many theories about how this was achieved. Chapter 3 examines Roman survey methods.

ERMINE STREET: THE FIRST GREAT NORTH ROAD

Many of the roads referred to above were already in place by the time London became prominent in the late first century, but the main route north appears to use

London as its starting point. Ermine Street left the north gate of the town and provided access to the legionary fortress at Lincoln. A major extension left the North Gate at Lincoln (now known as the Newport Arch), and travelled due north (the Humber was crossed by ferry), thus giving access to York. When the legion moved north to a more permanent base at the town, a direct route was established with Lincoln (now a *colonia*), thus avoiding the need for a ferry.

FOSS WAY: THE FIRST FRONTIER?

This road has long been a source of fascination. It appears to be an important road, carefully planned on a straight alignment, yet it emanates neither from Colchester nor London. It certainly provided a link between the legionary bases at Exeter and Lincoln, passing through important towns such as Bath, Cirencester and Leicester on the way. It has been suggested that, shortly after the invasion, the Romans decided that it was not necessary to push any further west and north, and built Foss Way to mark this frontier. A substantial line of forts, which would be expected for such a frontier (see below under Stanegate), has yet to be found. Perhaps a more likely explanation is that the road is an essential section of the road network, crossing and connecting the radial routes.

8. The North Gate of Vindolanda fort, Northumberland (NY 771664), showing the falling ground between it and Stanegate, the latter being flanked by the wall and tree-line beyond.

DERE STREET: FOLLOWING THE INVASION NORTHWARDS

This road represents the next phase of the invasion, carrying traffic initially to the line of forts on Stanegate (see below) and subsequently further into northern England and southern Scotland. The road was continually altered to take account of the varying policies that led to the building and abandonment of forts and walls. Dere Street was supplemented by a west coast road, which included a link to the important port of Ravenglass in Cumbria. These two roads, anchored at their southern ends by the two fortresses of York and Chester, must have had a pivotal role in the implementation of the many different policies adopted over time concerning the nature and position of the northern frontier.

STANEGATE: THE FIRST NORTHERN FRONTIER

This name applies to part of the road that crosses Great Britain from Carlisle to Corbridge, and may have continued to Newcastle, forming a sea to sea connection (see chapter 3 for the origin of the name). A number of forts and fortlets lie along the road: besides Corbridge, they include Carvoran, Haltwhistle Burn and *Vindolanda* at Chesterholm (figure 8). The road seems to make minor diversions from its straight course to pass close to the forts, so it was probably contemporary with them.

MILITARY ROADS

The Military Roads (or Military Ways) lie close to the southern side of both Hadrian's Wall and the Antonine Wall. Their purpose was to enable supplies to reach

9. Stanegate, marked by the hedge-line from top right, passing to the north of Vindolanda fort, before turning north-west towards the camera viewpoint (NY 781669). But which came first, road or fort?

10. The Military Way south of the Antonine Wall, heading east into Rough Castle Roman fort, near Falkirk in southern Scotland (NS 845795). The agger shows as a slight hump in the ground straight ahead, while on the left is the electricity pylon which can be seen in the right-centre foreground of figure 11.

the forts that were an integral part of both walls. In contrast to Stanegate and most other Roman roads, these roads often follow a twisting course as they were required to pass as near as possible to each fort (many of which are located on prominent high ground) while avoiding excessive gradients (figures 10, 11, 12 and 13).

THE WESTERNMOST ROADS

Surprisingly there is no sign of Roman road construction in Cornwall, despite the presence of some forts and mining activity. The most westerly roads are found in Wales. One road ran along the south coast from the legionary base at Caerleon, through Cardiff to Carmarthen; it continued westwards, certainly as far as Whitland and possibly on to St David's Head. Sarn Helen continued the coastal route that extended round to Chester, the legionary base that took over from Wroxeter. These two centres are linked to Caerleon by Watling Street (West). Thus there is a circuit of roads round Wales, which was supplemented by cross routes linking an internal network of forts (figure 14).

THE NORTHERNMOST ROAD

The Antonine Wall, across the Forth–Clyde isthmus, was not the most northerly fortified line. A road ran from the Wall along the Gask Ridge, with a series of forts and signal stations beside it. The largest of these was a full legionary fortress at Inchtuthil, built during Governor Agricola's campaigns in Scotland in the late first century, though the whole structure was dismantled again before it was occupied. The road ran beyond

11. *An aerial photograph of Rough Castle Roman fort, on the Antonine Wall near Falkirk, southern Scotland (NS 845795). The mound and ditch of the Wall can be seen entering the picture from the bottom centre, while the course of the Military Way, which follows the Wall to the south, enters the fort past the electricity pylon that can be seen in the right-centre foreground. (Crown Copyright RCAHMS)*

modern Perth, and ended at Kirriemuir. Recent research has suggested that, during the Agricolan advance, the road was probably rather insubstantial, whereas it was built to a much more solid form around the time of the Antonine advance in the mid second century. This might suggest that, for several years, the Romans had every intention of making the Gask Ridge a permanent frontier line (figures 15 and 16).

TOWN STREETS: SOME CURIOUS LAYOUTS

The streets of Roman towns are often thought to be laid out in a rigid grid pattern, akin to that now adopted by many towns in America. Two main streets, at right angles to each other, pass straight through the town, each entering through one gate and leaving through the opposite one, with minor streets crossing at right angles.

12. The Military Way, the supply road that runs just south of Hadrian's Wall, descending a slope, via a rock cutting, as it heads west from near Turret 39A (NY 756674).

13. View looking north to the South Gate of Milecastle 39 on Hadrian's Wall, close to the line of the road that led up to the gate from the Military Way (NY 762678).

This certainly seems to apply to the large Roman town of *Verulamium*, near St Albans (figures 17 and 18). But take a closer look at figure 17. The town lies on one of the most important roads in Roman Britain, Watling Street, and while one street certainly does pass straight between opposite gates, from north-west to south-east, Watling Street itself does not. The road certainly has high status within the town:

14. *Valley of the Afon Ogwen, Gwynedd, North Wales (SH 646661), viewed from the Nant Ffrancon Pass, looking north towards Bethesda. It has been suggested that a Roman road followed the valley on its way from the fort at Caer Llugwy, near Capel Curig, to the coast near Bangor, to assist in subduing the island of Anglesey. A likely course for the road is to the west (left) of the river, an alignment that is shared by several more recent tracks and turnpike roads. The modern A5 can be seen on the opposite side of the valley, using the dramatic terrace built by Thomas Telford in the nineteenth century, to avoid the steep gradients from which all the earlier routes suffered.*

it approaches from London, entering and leaving through large gates, and is provided, along its course through the town, with three large, triumphal arches. Yet anyone travelling along it would need to negotiate a series of right-angle turns to reach the centre and proceed along the same road.

The key probably lies in the fact that towns were planned not only to provide efficient traffic movement but also to give a good impression to visitors. Impressive gatehouses and town walls were as much to do with showing off a town's wealth and status as they were with defence alone. Within the town the street system was designed to bring visitors to the town's most prominent building, the basilica, perhaps equivalent to a modern town hall and law court combined.

The basilica occupied one side of the forum, an area that was enclosed on the other sides by shops and other business premises, and was often fronted by an impressive colonnade. Many towns were arranged such that travellers on their most

15. The most northerly Roman road, running along the Gask Ridge in Perthshire (NO 009206). Though only followed by a minor road today, this must have been an important route for the Roman army during its various attempts to occupy southern Scotland.

important road would arrive in front of the town's basilica, before continuing through the town or heading off to one side. This probably explains why Watling Street takes its rather indirect course through *Verulamium*. The same pattern can be seen in Roman London – for visitors crossing the important Thames bridge from the south – and in Silchester, where the street from London went through to the front of the forum.

16. The Roman road running east along the Gask Ridge, near Trinity Gask, Perthshire (NN 985197). In the foreground the Roman road is followed by a forest track, but is then joined by the minor road that can be seen entering at the bottom right of the picture. (Crown Copyright RCAHMS)

Here, however, a later change diverted the road from London past the forum to the north. Silchester has been the subject of intensive study since Victorian times, but new revelations continue to arise from current archaeological research. It appears that there was a grid of streets, or tracks, dating from the Iron Age, which was set at approximately forty-five degrees to the Roman layout; some inhabitants continued to build houses on this 'old' grid, even after the new one was in place.

At Wroxeter, Watling Street does not seem to have retained its status at all. The road can be seen entering the town from the north-east (bottom left of figure 19) on a curving alignment. Originally it led straight into the legionary fortress, probably through an impressive gateway, but after the fortress was demolished, it ended its long route from Kent on a comparatively narrow minor street. Its status was

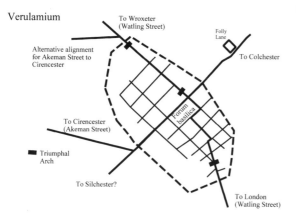

17. Diagram showing the street layout of the Roman town of Verulamium, near St Albans, Hertfordshire (TL 131078). Note the indirect course for the important Roman road, Watling Street.

superseded by Watling Street (West): though carrying a similar name it is another road entirely, and can be seen passing straight through the town (from bottom right to top left in the illustration). The road came to prominence as a link between the two fortresses of Chester and Caerleon, and it may have been traffic on this road,

18. Watling Street as it approaches the London Gate of Verulamium, St Albans, Hertfordshire (TL 136073). At this point the road uses a causeway to cross the deep town ditch, still a major feature beyond the railings on the right.

19. An artist's reconstruction of the Roman city of Wroxeter, Shropshire, as it may have looked in the third century (SJ 549087). By this time the legionary fortress that was originally on this site had moved to Chester, and the town had then developed as an important civil settlement. It lay astride the main north–south road, Watling Street (West), linking Chester to the other important western fortress at Caerleon. The road can be seen in the lower right of the picture as it approached from the north. The main line of Watling Street also entered the town, having crossed England from Richborough in Kent; it can be seen in the lower left of the picture, approaching from the north-east. (Photograph © English Heritage Photo Library)

rather than Watling Street, which helped Wroxeter to become one of the most prominent towns in Roman Britain.

Traffic in towns could be quite heavy, judging by the amount of maintenance that was needed (see chapter 3). There would have been a mix of military and civilian activity, with people on foot, on horseback and driving freight wagons. Priority would have been afforded to the high-status Imperial messenger service, the *cursus publicus*; its members rode on horseback or in light horse-drawn wagons, and merited official accommodation in a *mansio*, often a prominent building in Roman towns.

3

PLANNING AND CONSTRUCTION

THE PURPOSE OF ROMAN ROADS

THIS chapter looks at the two aspects of Roman roads that have made them famous: their directness and strength. How were they built, and, perhaps as important, why? After all, this was a settled land, with numerous tracks to allow people, animals and goods to move around, so why go to the trouble of building an entirely new network?

The Romans had thought through all that was required to occupy and govern a new province. Soldiers, supplies and equipment needed to be moved quickly to where they were needed, communications had to be as direct and reliable as possible, and government officials needed a safe way to move around the territory they were administering. The existing roads were just well trodden earth tracks winding between local settlements, pastures and mining sites, often unmarked and impassable in bad weather. A set of routes was needed to link the important centres directly, without diverting through intermediate settlements. Furthermore, the roads needed to be strong enough to support wagon wheels, even in wet weather – something the existing earth tracks could not do.

There is also a less tangible reason. In order to govern an area, you need to understand its geography. Good solid roads, with milestones to indicate distances, provided an unambiguous basis for this understanding. Once they are in place, roads can be used as the baselines for maps and boundaries, such as the Peutinger Table described in chapter 1.

The section looks at theories of how the Romans achieved their straight, direct alignments; the use of milestones, both as markers and as Imperial propaganda; and the methods of construction needed to withstand the wear from heavy wagons.

MAKING THE ROADS STRAIGHT

Next time you are out in the country, try to work out the direction of the nearest town without using a map, existing roads or a compass. Geographical features such as rivers, hills and tree-lines can help, but it is very difficult to establish the precise direction to a place, even just a few kilometres away, as soon as you are out of direct line of sight. This is precisely what the Roman road designers achieved over long distances, but the lack of any surviving Roman written accounts means that we have to make an educated guess as to how they did it.

There have been some exotic suggestions, such as the use of homing pigeons to indicate the required direction, but most modern theories advocate a sort of trial-and-error method, in which an approximate line for the road is adjusted successively until it is straight (see the upper diagram in figure 20). While this approach could be used for ironing out minor errors in local areas, it is quite impracticable over ten, let alone 100 kilometres; it is impossible to tell how to move the line in a specific place so as to bring it nearer to an overall straight line, and a lot of time and effort could be wasted in making the attempt.

ALTERNATIVE METHOD OF FINDING A STRAIGHT ROAD ALIGNMENT

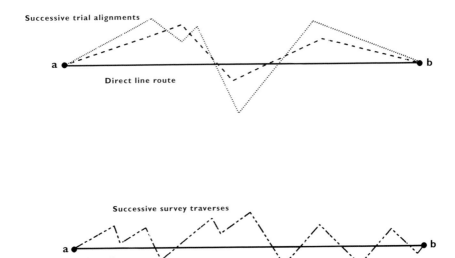

20. *Diagram showing alternative suggestions for the method used by Roman engineers to design a direct route from a to b. Upper: successively straightening a trial alignment; lower: using ground surveys to draw up a map, which can then be used to design the alignment.*

21. *Roman road from Winchester (Margary 45a), near Ford, Wiltshire (SU 162340), as it heads directly towards the Iron Age hill fort of Old Sarum.*

One might expect the Romans to have used a more straightforward method. Although they had no telescopes or magnetic compasses, they certainly did have a long tradition of complex surveying methods for measuring and laying out plots of land. There are also contemporary accounts of how to work out the direction and slope of a tunnel so that it joins two points on opposite sides of a mountain. Keeping these skills in mind we can work out a possible method for Roman road design.

The most likely answer is that, before any road was planned in detail, surveyors would produce a map or plan of the area through which the road was to pass. This could be done by surveyors walking the area, starting and finishing at the required end points of the road, and recording distance and direction as they went. (If each change of direction turns through a right angle, it is relatively easy to add up all the movements in one direction, and all those at right angles to it, and then use simple geometry to work out the bearing of the finish point relative to the start (see the lower diagram in figure 20). Along the way, other important features, such as rivers, forests, bogs and hills, could be recorded, and all the information drawn on a simple map, which could then be used by the road designers to plan an alignment. The road could be planned to link the end points as directly as possible, taking account of river crossings, soft ground or steep terrain in between. Unlike the trial-and-error method, this approach could be used over any distance. Furthermore, there could be several, independent surveying parties working simultaneously on different areas of land; provided those working on adjacent areas included an agreed common point in their respective surveys, their work could be combined afterwards. Subsequently, of course, this map could be dispensed with, because the road itself could be used as a baseline for a more accurate map, such as the Peutinger Table (see chapter 1), to aid military and civilian administrators, as well as travellers, in the future (figures 21 and 22).

22. Portway, between Silchester and Old Sarum, as it passes to the south of the Iron Age hill fort of Quarley Hill, Wiltshire (SU 262422). The alignment demonstrates that Roman road surveyors did not always align their roads directly towards high points in the landscape.

23. In situ *Roman milestone near the North Gate of* Vindolanda *fort, Chesterholm, Northumberland (NY 772665). The lack of an inscription may be because of weathering. Stanegate lies to the south (right), though separated from the stone by a post-Roman hedge-line.*

MILESTONES

Roman milestones were much more than merely indicators of distance from one town to the next, because they included a dedication to the Roman emperor who was in power at the time when the stone was placed, and stated the number of years he had reigned. This gives us a precise date for the placing of the stone, suggesting when the road was built or repaired. However, the use of the emperor's name also places milestones into a political context. They are in effect part of the propaganda process: a new Roman emperor could stamp his authority throughout the empire, by having new stones proclaiming his emperorship erected alongside, or even replacing, those of his predecessors. This was often done without the need for any proclamation or instruction, because all those who were responsible for roads in the vast empire-wide network were anxious to show they were in tune with the new regime in Rome.

Thus, potentially, milestones can tell us a good deal about how a Roman province reacted to the arrival of a new emperor. Unfortunately, in Britain we are hampered in realising this potential by the small number of milestones that have survived. Only just over a hundred are known, out of the many thousands that must have been erected, and of this small number only a tiny fraction are still in their original positions (figures 23 and 24 show two interesting examples near *Vindolanda*). Many of the rest have been incorporated into buildings, a process which actually began late in the Roman period. Such stones can be recognised by their characteristic inscriptions, sometimes only revealed when the building is being demolished. Other stones were simply discarded, lying unnoticed until discovered and studied by antiquarians or archaeologists. Some of these have found their way to museums; Chesters Museum has a group of five found

24. In situ *base of a Roman milestone, one Roman mile west of* Vindolanda *fort, Chesterholm, Northumberland (NY 757663). The remainder of the milestone, with an inscription, has been in use as a gatepost, nearby. The base lies beside Stanegate, followed by the modern minor road, passing to the right.*

near Stanegate. However, others have disappeared completely, known only from the written accounts left by their discoverers.

Most of the Roman milestones from Britain have been known for decades, even centuries (those now in Chesters Museum were discovered in 1885), so finding a formerly unknown one is rare. A welcome exception was the discovery in 1993 of the upper part of one, with its inscription intact, at Langwarthby in Cumbria.

STRUCTURE OF ROMAN ROADS

It is no accident that we know more about Roman roads than those that came earlier, or for over a thousand years later; their method of construction was stronger and more enduring than anything seen again until the eighteenth century. We have seen that the Romans needed good, well-defined roads as an essential aid to occupying and administering the province, but there is one other reason why the roads needed to be so strong, namely that the Romans had a tradition of using wheeled vehicles for moving heavy goods and equipment. Unprotected soil, though very resistant when dry, soon becomes soft when wet; one of the primary objectives of road-making was then, and still is, to provide a protective layer, called *metalling*, to spread the damaging impact of vehicle wheels so that the underlying soil is not damaged. Nowadays we use bitumen or concrete to provide a dense, cohesive layer, but in Roman times, and even until the twentieth century, loose stones or gravel served this purpose. Roman engineers' usual practice was to lay a foundation layer of larger stones, cobbles or pebbles, upon which was a surface layer of small stones or gravel (figures 25, 26 and 27). The hard, un-sprung wheels of wagons helped to compress the stones, breaking off small pieces and forcing them down between the larger stones to make a hard, smooth surface. In fact, so solid are some Roman road surfaces that they are hard to penetrate even with a pickaxe; this perhaps explains why digging through a Roman road is one of the least sought-after jobs on an archaeological site.

There is a widespread, but mistaken, theory that the Romans used a four-layer method of construction: this may have arisen from a misreading of the work of Vitruvius, a famous Roman architect, who identifies four successive layers, identified from bottom to top as *statumen, rudus, nucleus* and *pavementum*, including the use of cement and progressively finer stones or other hard material, towards the top. Though these names are still quoted as the essential elements of Roman road design, it seems clear from the context of his writing that Vitruvius was describing the paved area surrounding a large building, rather than a road. The mistake probably first arose in 1622, when a French engineer, Nicholas Bergier, hoping to learn from Roman experience how to improve road-building in his own time, excavated a length of Roman road and identified four layers within it, which he associated with Vitruvius' four layers. In practice it seems clear that there is no such consistent pattern; much

ROMAN ROAD CROSS-SECTION

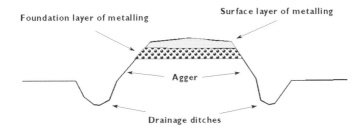

Foundation layer of metalling

Surface layer of metalling

Agger

Drainage ditches

25. Diagram of a 'typical' cross-section of a Roman road, showing the agger, drainage ditches and stone metalling. All these elements help to protect the underlying ground from damage by wheeled vehicles.

more common is the use of the two-layer structure described above. The four layers identified by Bergier were probably the result of an initial road, with a second one subsequently placed on top.

The Romans did not usually place metalling directly on the natural ground; they tended to dig ditches alongside, and to use the material in the middle to make

26. Wade's Causeway, the Roman road from Whitby, looking south towards Malton, photographed at a preserved section of metalling on Wheeldale Moor, near Goathland, North Yorkshire (SE 805975). Though the course of the road is uncertain beyond this point, it may well follow the minor road that can be seen in the distance.

33

27. *Wade's Causeway, the Roman road from Malton, looking north towards Whitby, photographed at a preserved section of metalling on Wheeldale Moor, near Goathland, North Yorkshire (SE 805975). The metalling is quite rough, and probably represents the foundation layer, somewhat disrupted by frost and erosion.*

28. Ackling Dyke, near Woodyates, Wiltshire (ST 018169), looking north-east towards Old Sarum. The agger *is still an impressive feature, nearly 2 metres high; in Roman times the road would have been kept clear of bushes and trees.*

29. Site of a probable Roman culvert on the line of Maiden Way, between Kirkby Thore and Carvoran, at Mere Sike, Cumbria (NY 676418). The culvert is partially collapsed, resulting in the stream finding an alternative route. (Photograph © John Howard)

30. Maiden Way, between Kirkby Thore and Carvoran, Cumbria, crossing a culvert (probably also of Roman origin) at Mere Sike (NY 676418). The culvert is partially collapsed but a slab, over a metre across, is still in place. (Photograph © John Howard)

31. Remains of a Roman ramp at Corbridge, Northumberland (NY 980646), which carried Dere Street down the steep south bank of the river Tyne to the bridge that carried traffic towards the Roman fort on the far side (looking west). (Photograph © Tyne and Wear Museum)

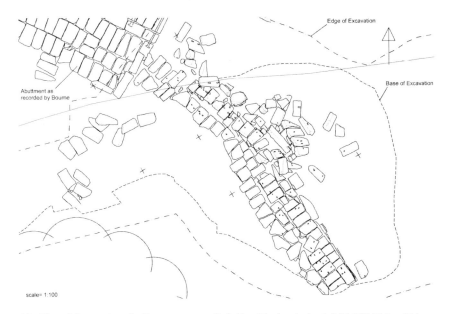

32. Plan of the remains of a Roman ramp at Corbridge, Northumberland (NY 980646), which carried Dere Street down the steep river bank to the bridge crossing of the Tyne. (Diagram © Tyne and Wear Museum)

a raised mound, called the *agger*, upon which the metalling was placed. This feature was not done just to make the road look impressive, which it certainly did on occasions (figure 28); the main purpose was to lower the water-table beneath the road in order to keep it as dry, and thereby as strong, as possible.

When rainwater is collected in ditches, it is carried to the nearest downhill watercourse, usually a stream. However, these watercourses can themselves cause problems when they cross the line of the road. The easiest solution is to allow the water to cross the road by means of a ford, perhaps with some stones beneath it to give a firm footing. Fords may be efficient but they can prove hazardous in wet weather to horse-riders, wagoners, and especially to people on foot. Fords also have the disadvantage of causing rapid wear and damage to the fabric of the road itself, often undermining any stones that are placed in the stream bed. Though there may have been many fords on the early Roman network, these were usually replaced by culverts, designed to carry the water beneath the road, thus keeping travellers dry and safe, and preserving the road fabric. Many of these culverts were solidly built of stone or brick, and still survive today (figures 29 and 30).

Sometimes the road needed to cross major rivers, which necessitated the use of ferries or bridges. Both the Humber, north of Lincoln, and the Severn, south of

Gloucester, were crossed by ferries throughout the Roman era, but many smaller rivers were crossed via stone or timber bridges. Unfortunately, traces of most of these have been lost, though remains have been found of a timber bridge over the Thames at Southwark, as have the footings and a ramp for a stone bridge over the Tyne at Corbridge (see figures 31–33).

Of course the roads needed regular maintenance, because wagon wheels and harsh weather conditions would disrupt the stones in the metalling over time. Each year stones would be replaced, and, when wear became too severe, with ruts beginning to appear, a complete new surface would be added, comprising a foundation and surface layer. In towns this process could be repeated ten times or more (figure 34).

The Romans seem to have been good at varying their approach to take account of local conditions. They used whatever stone was available, and varied the use of ditches and an *agger* depending on the quality of natural drainage in the area. In very boggy ground, brushwood might be used to fill the void, so that the road effectively floated on the surface.

The Roman approach to mountainous territory shows that, faced with difficult ground, they were prepared to adapt their design to fit the topography. Their mapping skills could suggest a direct route from start to finish, but such a route would often require extensive engineering, perhaps even including tunnels and high embankments. Though Roman engineers were quite capable of achieving these when necessary (there are fine examples in Italy), much simpler solutions were

33. Reconstruction of the Roman ramp at Corbridge, Northumberland (NY 980646), which carried Dere Street down the steep south bank of the river Tyne to access the bridge that carried traffic towards the Roman fort on the other side. Erosion of the river bank and flooding had caused part of the original structure to collapse, but silting had then preserved it. Further erosion uncovered the structure, but it needed to be removed to avoid further damage. The picture shows the original stones being re-erected further up the bank, to its original height of over 2.5 metres. (Photograph © Tyne and Wear Museum)

available provided some diversion was allowed. For example, terracing was used to provide a level, but curving, alignment for a road as it crossed a hillside, with culverts to carry water-courses beneath the road, and a ditch on the upper slope to carry water along to them. Many of these alignments are hard to find now because blockage of the culverts over intervening centuries has allowed water to build up on the upper side and wash the metalling down the slope.

When confronted with the need to climb steeply, the Romans would accept some quite steep gradients, perhaps 1 in 6. This would have needed careful

34. Section across the north–south street of Roman Silchester, covering the period between the first and third centuries. A succession of re-metalling treatments can be seen, each with a layer of pebbles forming a foundation, topped by a layer of gravel to provide the running surface.

35. *South-east Gate of Hardknott Roman fort, Cumbria (NY 218015). The Roman road from Ravenglass to Ambleside (Margary 740) passes just south of the fort (lower down the slope to the right). The modern road can be seen as it takes a zig-zag course up to Hardknott Pass; the Roman equivalent followed a very similar route.*

36. *A substantial cutting, up to 4.5 m deep, probably carrying a Roman road along the Gask Ridge, at Innerpeffray Library, near Perth, Scotland (NN 902184). Each side of the cutting was strengthened and waterproofed by a clay layer. A significant saving in construction effort was achieved by making the road wide enough for single-line traffic only. (Photograph © Dr D. J. Woolliscroft, University of Liverpool)*

negotiation by wagon-drivers, particularly on the descent, as braking systems were fairly primitive. For even steeper ground and long slopes, such as a mountain pass, the Romans favoured a zig-zag course, usually keeping the gradient to about 1 in 8, rather lower than was acceptable over shorter distances (figure 35).

Thus the Romans seem to have been sparing in the use of cuttings to lower the road gradient; three examples below describe this feature. The first cutting, at Innerpeffray Library, near Perth, Scotland, lies on the road that runs along the Gask Ridge, serving the most northerly line of Roman forts and signal stations in Britain (figure 36). At the point where the road has to climb a steep riverbank the road gradient has been kept to a minimum by the digging of a large cutting, up to 4.5 metres deep. It was a massive task, requiring the removal of over 1,900 cubic metres of material. This figure would have been over 50 per cent higher if the engineers had not decided to keep the road to a width suitable for single-line traffic only. A cutting this deep is vulnerable to weakening by rainwater penetration of the side slopes, making them unstable; this was countered by the Roman engineers, who plastered the cutting sides with puddled clay, making a waterproof revetment. Another substantial cutting was dug across Puddlehill in Hertfordshire; however, this has now been obscured by an even larger cutting that accommodates the modern A5 along the same course. Figure 37 shows a third example on very high ground in the Lake District; the road from Ambleside ascends to Hardknott Pass on a zig-zag course, and employs a cutting at the top as it passes a rocky outcrop.

On undulating ground, modern highway engineering practice often involves the construction of cuttings on hills, using the material dug out to form

37. *The raised* agger *of the Roman road from Ravenglass to Ambleside (Margary 740), near the summit of Hardknott Pass, Cumbria, looking west (NY 225014). Ahead is a small rock cutting, before the Roman road joins the modern one to descend rapidly towards Hardknott fort, out of sight below.*

embankments across valleys. This technique, though employed by the Romans in Italy, does not appear in Britain; indeed the high *agger* of Ackling Dyke is carried across hills as well as valleys (see figure 28 earlier in this chapter).

ROAD WIDTH: AN INDICATOR OF STATUS?

It is often thought that Roman roads have a standard width of 20 Roman feet. The Roman foot, the *pes* (plural *pedes*) is slightly shorter than an Imperial foot, at around 11½ inches (0.296 metres). This refers to the width that is provided with stone metalling and is thus available for wheeled traffic. The full width is usually greater than this, to accommodate side slopes of the *agger*, ditches and occasionally un-metalled strips beyond the main drainage ditches. Twenty feet would be an adequate width for most purposes, allowing wagons to pass each other in opposite directions, with some distance to spare.

In practice, however, the width of Roman roads can vary quite considerably between roads, and even along the same road. The average width for a number of well-known roads is as follows (in *pedes* with equivalent width in metres shown in brackets):

Watling Street	34 (10.1)	Dere Street	26 (7.7)
Ermine Street	29 (8.6)	Stane Street	25 (7.4)
Stanegate	26 (7.7)	Foss Way	18 (5.2)

These figures are derived from numerous excavations that have taken place along these roads over the past hundred years or so. They demonstrate that many roads are on average more than 20 *pedes* wide, with Watling Street seemingly the widest. One of the widest stretches of road is on Ermine Street, north of Lincoln, where the section running due north to the ferry crossing on the Humber averages 42 *pedes* (12.5 metres); this width is also evident on the more direct route from Lincoln to York. Even greater widths can be found in particular locations: at the point where the Great Road from London to Colchester crosses the River Lea at Old Ford, there are several parallel metalled lanes that have a total width of 59 *pedes* (17.5 metres). At the other extreme, Foss Way is only just over half the width of Watling Street.

Though traffic considerations can account for some variation in width, it seems unlikely that, outside towns, there would have been sufficient demand for very wide roads. Military power and status may offer a better explanation.

There are historical examples of roads being built very wide to allow for the rapid movement of troops, whether it be to enable twelve fully armed knights to ride side by side along the King's roads in medieval England, or for Napoleon III's troops to quell riots in the streets of Paris. Perhaps the Roman planners foresaw the need for particularly rapid movement across Britain along Watling Street; it was after all along this route that the Roman Governor Suetonius Paullinus had to move his troops from his military campaign against the Druids in Anglesey, to quell Boudicca's uprising. The memory of this event may have influenced the width of Watling Street, and others such as the major northern route, Ermine Street.

Many roads are fairly narrow, such as minor town streets or those providing local access to villas or small settlements. However, it might seem surprising if, as was noted earlier, Foss Way really was a major frontier, that its width is well below that of the other prominent routes. Occasionally a road may have been made narrower to save on construction costs, such as in the example we have already seen of the deep cutting at Innerpeffray (see figure 36 above). The same technique may also have been employed on Stane Street near Bignor in West Sussex, to enable the road to be built along the steep side of a narrow ridge. Certainly the existing road is extremely narrow, hardly wide enough for one line of wagons, let alone two (figure 38). While erosion has probably caused some damage, it seems unlikely that there was ever a wide road on this site. Single-line traffic over a significant length of road would have caused much inconvenience, so it is possible that Roman engineers built a second, parallel carriageway, further down the slope, to carry traffic in the opposite direction, and that this has been obliterated by erosion.

As many parts of Britain came to accept the Roman occupation, roads that had been built particularly wide for military purposes carried that status forward into civilian life, so that it became desirable to live near them and to develop those towns that lay along them.

38. *Stane Street (SU 991140), passing near Bignor Roman villa in West Sussex. The* agger *of the road is curiously narrow at this point, possibly caused by erosion, or because the road was split into two carriageways as it crossed the hillside.*

4

ROMAN ROAD NAMES

MANY Roman roads have names, some of which are extremely well known, such as Watling Street and Foss (or Fosse) Way (see Appendix 3 for a list of the principal road names). Such names are useful for identification, and often give, in addition, an air of romance. The main problem with them is that they do not date from the Roman era itself; surprisingly perhaps, there is practically no evidence of what the Romans called their roads in the province of *Britannia*. It is possible that there were equivalents of the *via Appia* or *via Flaminia*, two of the major roads leading into Rome, which carried the name of those who sponsored their construction or to whom they were dedicated. Roads in Britain may have had names that were more directly related to their destination, such as the *via Londinium*. None of the few contemporary Roman documents refers to road names, and no milestones have survived that refer to them either. What we do have is a set of names that derive from the Anglo-Saxon and Norse invaders, who arrived after the legions were withdrawn and Britain effectively left the Roman Empire. The new occupiers were aware of the roads, many of which were, of course, major features in the landscape. Anglo-Saxon *stræte* and Norse *gate* begin to appear on land charters, using a stretch of Roman road as a local boundary-marker. Gradually, over the next century or so, names were applied to longer stretches of Roman road. For example, Watling Street began as *Wæclinga stræte*, that is, the road leading to the land of the *Wæclingas*, probably a local tribe or family living near St Albans. This eventually became Watling Street, and applied to the whole route from the Kent coast at Richborough, through London and St Albans, and on to Wroxeter. A similar process gave rise to Foss Way (from the Latin for a ditch or bank), and Stane Street ('stane' probably comes from stone, referring to the stone metalling). Stanegate, running across Britain just south of Hadrian's Wall, has the same origin, but includes the Norse word 'gate', for road. Some names, such as Devil's Highway and Devil's Causeway, give a clue to the awe that the Roman alignments seem to have engendered (figure 39).

39. Devil's Highway (SU 876649), between Bagshot, Surrey and Crowthorne, Berkshire, looking west. The prominent agger at this point may have given rise to its name in the Anglo-Saxon period.

There are several confusing elements associated with these traditional, though non-Roman names. Akeman, King, Stane, Stone and Watling are each applied to more than one completely different road. Also, there is Ermine Street, from London to Lincoln, and Ermin Street, from Silchester to Gloucester. More confusion can arise from the use of different spellings for the same road; Foss(e) Way and Rykni(e)ld Way seem to be interchangeable.

Some roads have names which sound genuinely 'Roman' such as the *via Devana*, from Godmanchester to Colchester. However, these are likely to be much more recent inventions. In the early modern period, antiquarians began to explore the newly discovered Roman network, and attached plausible-sounding names based on some supposed historical connection.

There is one name that can lay claim to a possible origin during the Roman occupation, associated with places in Wales using the word *Sarn* (Welsh for 'causeway'). There are two Roman roads in Wales called Sarn Helen, supposedly

45

named after a British princess who married the Roman Emperor Maximus, and who was said to have caused the roads to be built. There are other places in Wales with 'Sarn' in their names, often with a Roman road nearby. Although the legend of Helen does not appear in written form until the medieval *Mabinogion* was written down, it almost certainly had a much earlier origin, passed down in an oral tradition. The legend relates to the Roman period, so perhaps the use of 'Sarn' in road names does too.

MARGARY NUMBERS

Only a minority of Roman roads have traditional names, and even when such a name is known, there can be confusion about how far along a particular route the name applies. Fortunately nearly all of them have been given a number, often accompanied by a letter. This numbering system is the work of Ivan Margary, an indefatigable antiquarian who traced thousands of miles of Roman roads during the early and mid twentieth century. It uses roughly the same convention as the modern road network, with more important roads having single digits, those in between having two, and minor ones three. Letters apply to different sections of the same road. Useful though these numbers undoubtedly are, they can be misleading. The fact that different sections of a road all have the same number gives the impression that the Romans considered it to be a single, long road. Because we do not have original Roman names, we have to rely on history, geography and archaeology to suggest which lengths go together. Such evidence is often ambiguous, so Margary's numbers, and even the traditional names, should be regarded as a useful means of identification, rather than as an indication of what the Roman policy was when the roads were originally built. Appendix 3 shows the Margary numbers for roads that also have traditional names; a full list can be found in books by Margary himself or by the present author (see chapter 7).

5

ROMAN ROADS SINCE ROMAN TIMES

As we have seen, the famous names that Roman roads carry are the legacy of the Anglo-Saxons and Danes, but the existence of the names may give a misleading impression of how the roads were used following the end of the occupation. The society that replaced the Romans was, for several centuries, much more like that which had existed before the Roman legions invaded, namely a mainly rural, tribal society, with little use for long-distance travel and no tradition of wheeled vehicle transport. But so prominent were the roads left behind by the Romans that they remained a permanent feature of the landscape; even if they were not used as tracks, the *agger*s were used as boundaries and frontiers. Even now parish boundaries often follow such routes. Clearly many did retain their use as tracks – otherwise they would not still be in use today – but little attempt was made to maintain them. Archaeological evidence often shows a layer of earth on top of Roman metalling underneath the road surface laid down in the modern or early modern era.

New settlements began to grow again, and towns reappeared, often in locations un-served by the Roman network. A process of adaptation began, as the network adjusted to serve the new settlements, with fresh tracks appearing, and others veering away from Roman roads, only to rejoin the Roman line further on. By about the thirteenth century, a network of roads and lanes, part Roman, part post-Roman, had evolved, which remained largely unchanged into the motor era. Enclosure, and the turnpike roads, added some new routes and modified others, but an essentially medieval network survived until the motor era demanded that roads be made straighter and flatter, a process that is still going on.

However, the medieval roads were not metalled, apart from a few city streets; there were few wagons since most people walked or rode on horseback, and goods were carried by pack animals. Although medieval bridges were prominent, and sometimes still remain in use, the roads between them were generally poor by Roman standards.

The use of the names given to Roman roads suggests that they carried a strong tradition. Medieval writers tend to ascribe them to the ancient British, rather than to the Roman invaders. Four of the roads carried legal status: Ermine Street, Watling Street, Foss Way and Icknield Street were called 'The Four Great Roads', upon which travellers could expect the King's protection. However, there was no official description of where these roads went, and medieval writers disagree about their precise course, so it would have been hard for a medieval traveller to be sure they were entitled to royal protection, even if there were a method of enforcing it.

In the Tudor period, prosperity began to rise, and with it the volume of road traffic. Wheeled carts and wagons for goods, and carriages for people, began to use the roads; un-metalled surfaces that had coped well enough with hooves and feet began to deteriorate. Engineers in France realised that there was, beneath the ground, evidence of superior road-making techniques, and they attempted to copy what appeared to be the Roman technique of metalling. Unfortunately this resulted in an over-complicated design, because what had been unearthed was the result of centuries of repair and re-making, rather than an original road design. Nevertheless, the eighteenth century saw the beginning of a careful study of Roman roads, in Britain and elsewhere, with

40. The top surface of the north–south street of Roman Silchester (Calleva Atrebatum) (SU 640625), with the North Gate indicated by the gap in the town wall at the far end. The photograph was taken in 1999, the third season of the University of Reading's excavation of Insula IX. Note the short depth of the road surface below the present-day ground surface, resulting from the abandonment of the town after the Roman period.

41. The north–south street of Roman Silchester in 2007, the tenth year of excavation. Besides using the excavation for research and training, the University of Reading attracts progressively more public interest during its open days. The road surface of this part of the street has been reduced to the third-century level, although elsewhere on the site first-century remains have been reached.

antiquarians such as William Stukeley following and illustrating their courses. This process of enquiry and discovery is still going on, with hundreds of excavations encountering sections of Roman road to add further knowledge (figures 40 and 41).

Though antiquarians and engineers in the seventeenth and eighteenth centuries used the remains of Roman roads as a model for their own road-building, Victorian archaeologists saw that the roads (and particularly town streets) offered clues to the location of buildings, which in turn might lead to dramatic mosaics, jewellery or well-preserved pottery items. Until recently, roads were seen as an unexciting element in an excavation: having located some metalling, and identified it as probably Roman (because of its structure, location or occasionally from dating evidence), the excavators have tended to concentrate on what lies beside the road. Modern archaeological techniques have led to greater awareness of what a road can contribute to wider knowledge: how wide it is gives an indication of its importance, while the number of repairs suggests the volume of traffic that used it. If changes to the road can be dated from items found within the structure, these can sometimes be correlated with historical events, such as the reoccupation of a fortress, the expansion of a town, or perhaps the temporary abandonment of a settlement because of flooding or fire.

Improvements in the excavation approach have occurred in tandem with the development of non-destructive techniques, such as soil resistivity measurement and ground-penetrating radar, both of which can give an increasingly accurate picture of what lies beneath the soil. These can often be used to confirm the presence of road metalling or ditches. Another technique that is particularly useful for locating roads and streets is aerial survey. Crop-marks can indicate the position of metalled surfaces and ditches, while the straight course of existing roads or tracks that follow Roman roads can be dramatically illustrated (see figures 42 and 43).

42. The Roman road from Chichester, entering the South Gate of Roman Silchester, Hampshire (SU 630613), to become the main north–south street. This passed straight through the town between the South and North Gates; its course, along with that of other streets within the walled area, is revealed by light-coloured crop-marks. (Copyright reserved Cambridge University Collection of Air Photographs)

43. *The A1198, south of Huntingdon, following the line of Roman Ermine Street (TL 280642). This section of the Roman line remained the main route for the Great North Road until the turnpike era of the eighteenth century, when it was replaced by the modern A1. (Copyright reserved Cambridge University Collection of Air Photographs)*

Advances in non-destructive methods are leading to a growing view that archaeological remains should, if possible, be left undisturbed, in the hope that, in the future, they can be fully understood without the need to destroy them by excavation. Two sorts of excavation do still take place however: the most common, usually termed 'rescue' archaeology, is carried out when planned development would otherwise destroy any archaeological remains lying beneath the ground; less common are 'research' digs, where permission is granted for an academic institution or society to study a particular site over a long period. Research excavations provide a training ground for future archaeologists and, in addition, give good opportunities for public access (see figures 40 and 41 earlier in this chapter).

51

6

ROMAN ROADS IN THE MODERN LANDSCAPE

G IVEN the pressure of modern development, and the need for more and wider roads, it may seem improbable that a network of roads built two thousand years ago has retained any influence at all on the modern landscape. Yet some modern

44. *Roman Dere Street, looking south near Manfield, North Yorkshire (NZ 216143). Though followed only by a minor road at this point, the Roman line is taken up by the A1, beyond the kinks in the line which can be seen at the top of the picture. (Copyright reserved Cambridge University Collection of Air Photographs)*

roads, large or small, tracks, paths, field and parish boundaries or even just lines of trees, attest to this ancient system. As we have seen, changing settlement patterns in medieval times necessitated changes to the Roman network, but many lengths of Roman road appear to have been in more or less continuous use ever since (figure 44) Large towns, such as London, Chester, Lincoln and York, re-established

45. *Present-day Ancaster, Lincolnshire (SK 982434) lies on a minor road that follows the line of Ermine Street, the main Roman road from London to Lincoln. The settlement had Iron Age origins before becoming a Roman fort and defended town (centred round the present-day church, to the left of the road in the foreground, and the field opposite). In medieval times the main northbound route, the Great North Road (modern A1), moved 15 kilometres to the west, with York as its destination rather than Lincoln. (Copyright reserved Cambridge University Collection of Air Photographs)*

themselves on the Roman road network, though their street layouts often differed from those of their Roman predecessors. This may have been because the hard metalled Roman surfaces made ideal foundations for medieval houses, while the un-metalled spaces in between were good enough for streets. Large numbers of smaller towns originated as roadside settlements along open stretches of road, to serve travellers with refreshment, accommodation and goods (figure 45). Their main streets often still follow the Roman line, albeit now carrying local traffic only, as through-traffic is normally served by a bypass.

Long stretches of roads such as the A68 (Dere Street), north and south of Hadrian's Wall, the A5 (Watling Street) in Hertfordshire, and the 'old' line of A417 and A419 (Ermin Street) between Swindon and Gloucester, and passing through Cirencester, still follow the Roman line. By contrast, Silchester and Wroxeter, both of which were major towns and important centres in the Roman road network, have completely vanished, to be replaced (in medieval times) by Reading and Shrewsbury respectively.

In mountainous areas, such as west and north Wales, it is far more difficult to trace the Roman line. Often there is a limited range of possible courses for a road in the area, so prehistoric tracks, Roman roads and medieval routes may all occupy the same course.

46. Paved street of the vicus *(civil settlement) outside the west gate of* Vindolanda *Roman fort, Chesterholm, Northumberland (NY 771664).*

47. *Drainage channel, alongside the paved street of the* vicus *(civil settlement) outside the west gate of* Vindolanda *Roman fort, Chesterholm, Northumberland (NY 771664).*

55

When there is some doubt about whether or not a particular feature is genuinely Roman, archaeologists look for dating evidence, in the form of coins or pottery fragments, dropped accidentally when the road was being built, or during its use. Unfortunately only about 10 per cent of excavations actually produce dating evidence, so it is usually the case that something which looks Roman (because it is straight and lies where a Roman road might be expected to be) and 'feels' Roman (because young archaeologists have a hard time digging into it) can be assumed to be Roman. After all, it was over a thousand years before roads began to be built in the same way again.

But mistakes can be made. Famous lengths of supposedly Roman road, such as the Dean Road in the Forest of Dean and Blackstone Edge between Manchester and Ilkley Moor, are probably of early modern origin. The former may have been built as a philanthropic means of providing employment, while the latter, comprising an extremely steep paved surface, may have been an inclined plane wagon-way, built in the turnpike era. Blackstone Edge has often been cited as a demonstration that the whole of the Roman road network was originally paved with large slabs of stone. Archaeology has shown that very few areas were paved, and where they were, it was more for show and status than for practical road-making.

Roman road metalling itself can usually be viewed only when an excavation is taking place (see figures 40 and 41 above), but lengths are sometimes left open for us to inspect at any time. For example, a length of Foss Way can be seen through a glass panel in the floor of St Mary's Guildhall in Lincoln, and visitors to Wheeldale Moor in North Yorkshire can walk along a section of Wade's Causeway (see figures 26 and 27 above). In each of these preserved sections, it is probably the foundation layer which can be observed, the running surface of gravel having long since been dispersed by wear and weathering. For the most part, the actual Roman metalling, assuming it survived ploughing and stone robbing over the centuries, lies buried under soil or modern road material.

EXPLORING ROMAN ROADS

Most people's experience of Roman roads probably derives from driving along a straight stretch of modern road that follows the Roman course, such as the A68 north of Hadrian's Wall. The road follows the line of Dere Street on a dead straight alignment through undulating terrain. While this switchback course can be exhilarating to drive along, there are hidden dangers when oncoming vehicles 'disappear' into hollows, tempting people to overtake at inappropriate times. More leisurely enjoyment can be derived from following the course of a Roman road that is now only a minor road, a track or a path through the countryside. The illustrations in this book give examples of accessible sections of Roman road to visit, and chapter 9 looks at information covering present knowledge of the location of Roman roads.

However, this knowledge is continually being added to by new archaeological investigations. Usually these tend to confirm the presence of a known road, but occasionally doubt arises about even quite well known lengths of road. We have already mentioned two sites, Blackstone Edge and the Dean Road, which were thought to be Roman but which now seem more likely to be of much more recent origin. On the other hand there are sections of well-established routes that have yet to be located, and there are whole lengths of road that have long been proposed as Roman in origin, but for which there is, as yet, little direct evidence at all. Some of these are listed below:

A ROAD FROM LONDON TO WINCHESTER

Travellers from London to Winchester in Roman times appear to have needed to travel via Silchester, but a more direct route has long been postulated. William Stukeley toured England in the 1720s, and claimed to have ridden his horse along such a road, passing through Farnham. The only evidence that has arisen is the suggestion of a length of buried road near Staines, and the streets of a small Roman settlement at Neatham, near Alton, which could lie on such a road.

A ROAD FROM ST ALBANS TO SILCHESTER

A group called the Viatores has suggested a course for such a road, linking the important Roman towns of *Verulamium* and *Calleva*; this would include a Thames crossing near Cookham. Despite the fact that the south-west gate of *Verulamium* is traditionally called 'The Silchester Gate', no firm evidence of such a road has yet been confirmed.

THE ROAD TO ST DAVID'S, WEST OF CARMARTHEN

When Ivan Margary did his monumental study of Roman roads in the mid twentieth century, he was not aware of any route west of Carmarthen in south Wales. However, since then, direct evidence has shown a well-built road running due west, at least as far as Whitland. Aerial photographs suggest it may go further, perhaps as far as St David's Head.

DEVIL'S HIGHWAY, WEST OF STAINES

The important Roman road from London to Silchester crosses the Thames at Staines, and re-emerges at Virginia Water (figure 48), but its precise course between these points is uncertain. Incidentally, further west, there is a road south of Bracknell called Nine Mile Ride, which is often thought locally to be of Roman origin because of its straight alignment. As it happens, this is one point where the Roman line is well known, and lies several hundred metres to the south. Nine Mile Ride itself is probably, as its name implies, a 'ride' to allow a hunting party rapid movement through the Royal hunting forest, and dates from medieval or early modern times.

48. *The Devil's Highway, between London and Silchester, heading south-west into the park at Virginia Water, Surrey (SU 993695). The* agger *can still be discerned, though obscured by tree growth.*

8

CONCLUSIONS

THE Romans are rightly famous for their roads, which extended throughout their empire. This book has concentrated on the network that they constructed in Britain, during the nearly four centuries in which it belonged to the Roman Empire. By any standards it was an astonishing achievement: in both length and strength, the Roman network is comparable with Britain's motorway and trunk road system combined. Almost all the expertise for this work came with the legions; although the island of Britain was settled throughout, the transport network comprised little more than a series of local, unmade tracks. These were entirely adequate for the movement of animals to pasture and market, for the transport of mining products to the nearest river, and for the occasional deployment of war bands as the various tribes of Britain strove for supremacy. But, crucially, there were few wheeled vehicles, and there was no strategic vision of the island as a unified political entity.

All this changed when the legions landed in AD 43. In contrast to the two incursions by Julius Caesar a century earlier, the new arrivals were here to stay, and, as far as we can tell, had every intention of bringing the whole island under Roman control. Thus, from the start, their thinking was strategic. Indeed, there were battles and conflicts with some of the more hostile tribes, requiring many tactical decisions as time went on, but the Roman army immediately set about penetrating to the furthest corners of the land. The fact that, within a few decades of arriving, they were constructing a full legionary fortress north of the Forth–Clyde Isthmus, shows the scale of this ambition. The layout of roads reflected this thinking, for the alignments were designed to link important military and civilian sites 50 kilometres or more apart. They had the surveying skills to align such roads correctly, using as direct a route as possible, while making sensible adjustments to take account of topography.

Their method of construction was different too. Unmade tracks would not support the wheeled vehicles that the Roman army was accustomed to using; thick stone metalling provided a strong road structure while the raised *agger*, and the roadside ditches from which material for the *agger* was obtained, both contributed to keeping the underlying soil as dry, and therefore as strong, as possible.

However, such strong roads could take years to build; the army needed something in place much more quickly to keep supplies, troops and building materials moving up to the front line. Thus the first road structures, though well aligned, were probably built to a lower standard of construction, perhaps no more than a strip of cleared ground, shallow ditches and very light metalling. These early structures are hard to find, so it is the later, more solidly built constructions that are located by archaeologists. Disentangling the sequence of events can be difficult; some

49. *Section of the north–south street of Roman Silchester down to the first-century level. Alternating layers of foundation and surface can be discerned, the former characterised by pebbles and the latter by gravel. An anomalous layer is indicated, which may suggest that the road was not used for traffic at a period in the second or third centuries.*

of the roads seem more massive and complex than they were, because what we see in modern excavations may be the result of several phases of road-building. Archaeologists have found examples of not only a strong road on top of a flimsy one, but several strong roads one on top of the other, perhaps representing two or three hundred years of repairs and reconstruction (figure 49).

There can be another source of confusion: although there does not seem to have been any comparable road-building for over a thousand years after Roman occupation, the absence of direct dating can make it hard to say for sure that what has been found is not a road from the early modern era. Datable evidence, either from the road itself or from ditches or roadside features can sometimes help, and a further clue can lie in the presence of a layer of wind- or water-borne soil separating two metalled layers, indicating a long period of neglect.

The Roman road network has been a subject of interest amongst antiquarians and archaeologists for several centuries, resulting in the current awareness of the scale and reach of the network. All the main Roman towns, fortresses, ports and mining centres were served by major roads, while a whole series of new roadside settlements grew up to serve travellers (see figure 50, and also figure 45 in chapter 6). Wheeled vehicles were used for transporting heavy goods, building materials and supplies, though most people, whether military or civilian, still moved about on foot. For everyone, though, the new roads offered improved travel conditions, with straight predictable alignments that were clear of trees and other obstructions, milestones to mark out the route, and dry conditions underfoot.

For many archaeologists, once a section of road has been identified as of Roman origin, interest turns to what lies beside it. Yet we are now realising that there may also be valuable material hidden within the structure itself. The nature of the wear on the various layers, and even what material was used, can give clues about what was happening in the surrounding area, such as the start of a new military campaign or the development of a new mining or manufacturing centre. Within a town, the layers of street metalling may suggest which parts of the town were developing or declining at any given time (see figure 49).

The Roman road network has a more immediate impact on modern life than any other remains of the occupation, and can be enjoyed without the need for archaeology. After all, we cannot live in Roman villas, bathe in their bathhouses or shop in their markets, but we can travel along their roads. They were built to provide efficient routes for travellers, and many of them still do: modern roads, tracks or footpaths often continue to follow the alignments first set out by Roman engineers nearly two thousand years ago. This was Britain's first properly engineered transport system, and, although it is over fifteen hundred years since the legions left Britain's shores, their roads are, in many cases, still with us today.

50. High Street, Cowbridge, South Glamorgan (SS 986748). The street follows the line of the Roman road running west from Caerleon. The town had Roman origins as a settlement alongside the road, and was probably the site of a fort, intermediate between Cardiff and Neath.

FURTHER READING

Study of maps is probably the best starting point, and we are fortunate that in Britain the Roman roads are often clearly identified. All the Ordnance Survey *Explorer* and *Landranger* maps show the location of well-established Roman roads, and the entire network is shown on the Ordnance Survey *Map of Roman Britain*. This map also shows the modern road network to aid identification.

There are many other sources of information besides maps. A visit to the local museum at home or on holiday can show the best places to go in an area (a list of those which are particularly relevant to the Roman road network is given in the next chapter). For more detailed information it is best to have a look at one or more of the numerous books that cover the subject.

The most comprehensive description of the network is still Ivan Margary's *Roman Roads in Britain*, first published in two volumes in 1955 and 1956 by Phoenix House. The most recent edition, combined into a single volume, was published by John Baker in 1973. All editions are now out of print, but can be borrowed from libraries or purchased second-hand. Margary is the originator of the numbering system referred to in chapter 4, and he gives a detailed description of the course of over 10,000 kilometres (about 6,000 miles) of roads that he considers to be Roman. Unfortunately he does not give map references; nor does he state whether or not particular sections are accessible. A useful source for this information, or for a selection of sites at least, is provided by Helen Livingstone's *In the Footsteps of Caesar: Walking Roman Roads in Britain*, published in 1995 by Dial House. Many areas of Britain have been studied in detail by particular authors: for example, the north-west of England is covered by a series of books by Philip Grayson. Titles include *Walking Roman Roads in East Cumbria*, and *Walking Roman Roads in the Fylde and Ribble Valley*, published in 1994 and 1996 respectively by the Centre for North-West Regional Studies at Leicester University. The northern part of Wales is covered by *The Roman Roads of North Wales* by Edmund Waddelove, printed in 1999 by Gee and Son of Denbeigh, while the area around St Albans is covered in *Roman Roads in the South-East Midlands*, by The Viatores, and published by Gollancz in 1960. For a study of the engineering and historical background to Roman roads in Britain, and the history of roads in general, see *Roads in Roman Britain* and *From Trackways to Motorways: 5000 Years of Highway History*, by the present author and published by Tempus of Stroud in 2002 and 2006 respectively.

For those who want to go into more detail still on a particular road, perhaps the best course is to join a local archaeological society. Many of these have an active research group who may be taking an interest in the same route. Details of what has been found along a route can be obtained from the relevant county Sites and Monuments Record, while there are many descriptions and analyses contained in journal articles and notes. Two particularly useful sources are: the annual description of finds in Roman Britain, contained in the journal *Britannia*, published by the Society for the Promotion of Roman Studies; and the *Bibliography of British and Irish Archaeology* produced by the Council for British Archaeology. The former is produced in both printed and digital form, while the latter is now available as an open-access, on-line catalogue.

There are several sources of aerial survey photographs, some resulting from flights by the RAF (or from German planes during World War II) and the Ordnance Survey. Others have developed from particular projects, or are the work of dedicated individuals. English Heritage Photographic Library, NMRC, Kemble Drive, Swindon, SN2 2GZ (PhotoLibrary@english-heritage.org.uk) and Cambridge University Aerial Photo Library, Unit for Landscape Modelling, Sir William Hardy Building, Downing Site, Cambridge (library@uflm.cam.ac.uk) are the main sources in England. Scotland and Wales are covered by collections held by the Royal Commission on the Ancient and Historical Monuments of Scotland, John Sinclair House, 16 Bernard Terrace, Edinburgh EH8 9NX (nmrs@rcahms.gov.uk) and The Royal Commission for Ancient and Historic Monuments in Cymru Wales, Plas Grug, Aberystwyth, Ceredigion SY23 1NJ (nmr.wales@rcahmw.org.uk).

LIST OF MUSEUMS

The following are some of the museums that illustrate Roman roads or streets in their locality.

Canterbury Roman Museum, Longmarket, Butchery Lane, Canterbury, Kent CT1 2JR. Telephone: 01227 785575. (Watling Street and town streets)

Chesterholm Museum (Vindolanda), Bardon Mill, Hexham, Northumberland NE47 7JN. Telephone: 01434 344277. Website: www.vindolanda.com (Stanegate, milestones, paved street of *vicus*)

Chesters Roman Fort Museum, Chollerford, Humshaugh, Hexham, Northumberland NE46 4EU. Telephone: 01434 681379. (Roman milestones)

Colchester Castle Museum, Castle Park, Colchester, Essex CO1 1TJ. Telephone: 01206 282939. Website: www.colchestermuseums.org.uk (Balkerne Gate and the Great Road)

The Collection, Danes Terrace, Lincoln LN2 1LP. Telephone: 01522 550990. (Streets and aqueduct). Also, *St Mary's Guildhall*, 385 High Street, Lincoln LN5 7SF. Telephone: 01522 546422. (Preserved section of Roman road – by appointment)

Corbridge Roman Fort Museum, Corbridge, Northumberland NE45 5NT. Telephone: 01434 632349. (Dere Street and Roman bridge ramp)

Corinium Roman Museum, Park Street, Cirencester, Gloucestershire GL7 2BX. Telephone: 01285 655611. (Foss Way, Ermin Street and Akeman Street)

Falkirk Museum, Falkirk FK2 9TD. (Military Way at Rough Castle Roman fort on Antonine Wall)

Museum of London, London Wall, London EC2Y 5HN. Telephone: 0870 444 3852. Website: www.museumoflondon.org.uk/English (Roman bridge and street scenes)

National Museum of Scotland, Chambers Street, Edinburgh EH1 1JF. Telephone: 0131 225 7534. Website: www.nms.ac.uk (Roman advances in Scotland)

National Museum of Wales, Cathays Park, Cardiff CF10 3NP. Telephone: 02920 397951. Website: www.museumwales.ac.uk (Development of Roman road network in Wales)

National Roman Legion Museum, High Street, Caerleon, Newport, South Wales NP18 1AE. Telephone: 01633 423134. Website: www.museumwales.ac.uk/en/caerleon (Fortress streets and approach roads)

Reading Museum, The Town Hall, Blagrave Street, Reading, Berkshire RG1 1QH. Telephone: 0118 939 9800. Website: www.readingmuseum.org.uk (Finds from Silchester)

Richborough Roman Fort Museum, Richborough, Kent CT13 8JW. Telephone: 01304 612013. (Great Monument and start of Watling Street)

Roman Army Museum, Greenhead, Northumberland CA6 7JB. Telephone: 01697 747485. (Military Way of Hadrian's Wall)

Tullie House Museum and Art Gallery, Castle Street, Carlisle, Cumbria CA3 8TP. Telephone: 01228 618718. Website: www.tulliehouse.co.uk

Tyne and Wear Museums, Discovery Museum, Blandford Square, Newcastle Upon Tyne NE1 4JA. Telephone: 0191 232 6789. Website: www.twmuseums.org.uk/discovery (Hadrian's Wall area)

Verulamium Museum, St Michael's Street, St Albans, Hertfordshire AL3 4SW. Telephone: 01727 751810. Website: www.stalbansmuseums.org.uk (Watling Street and town streets)

Wroxeter Roman City, Wroxeter, Shropshire SY5 6PH. Telephone: 01743 761330. (Watling Street and Watling Street (West))

Yorkshire Museum and Gardens, Museum Gardens, York, North Yorkshire YO1 7FR. Telephone: 01904 687687. Website: www.yorkshiremuseum.org.uk Also, *Roman Bath Museum*, St Sampsons, York. Telephone: 01904 620455. (Streets of Roman York)

APPENDIX 1: GLOSSARY

agger	The raised mound upon which Roman road-metalling was laid
basilica	High-status building along one side of the forum, housing the town's administration and judiciary
civitas	Roman town designated as a tribal capital
colonia	Civilian settlement replacing a fortress, peopled mainly by retired soldiers and their families
cursus publicus	Imperial messenger service
forum	The important business and administrative centre of a Roman town and the focus for the street network; it comprises a colonnaded square, with the basilica along one side
mansio	Well-appointed accommodation for travellers on important official business, such as members of the *cursus publicus*
metalling	Layers of stones to protect the soil beneath from the damaging effects of wheeled vehicles
revetment	Measures to maintain stability, such as masonry walls or waterproofing on the sides of a steep-sided road cutting
vicus	Civilian settlement outside the defences of a Roman fort or fortress

APPENDIX 2: INDEX OF PLACE NAMES

Throughout this book places have usually been referred to by their modern names for ease of reference. However, nearly all of these date from the Anglo-Saxon period; during the Roman occupation, quite different names were used, often of Celtic origin. Some town names were combined with the name of the local tribe, suggesting the awarding of *civitas* status as a tribal capital. Establishing the Roman name for a particular site may not be straightforward and many smaller sites, whether military or civilian, have no known Roman name at all. Where Roman names for places mentioned in the book have been established, they are listed below, with a question mark signifying some uncertainty.

Modern name	Roman name	*Modern name*	Roman name
Bath	*Aquae Sulis*	Gloucester	*Glevum*
Caerleon	*Isca*	Hardknott	*Mediobogdum*
Caernarfon	*Segontium*	Leicester	*Ratae Corieltavorum*
Caerwent	*Venta Silurum*	Lincoln	*Lindum*
Caistor St Edmond	*Venta Icenorum*	London	*Londinium*
Cambridge	*Duroliponte*	Neatham	*Onna?*
Canterbury	*Durovernum Cantiacorum*	Old Sarum	*Sorviodunum*
Carlisle	*Luguvalium*	Ravenglass	*Glannaventum*
Carmarthen	*Moridunum*	Richborough	*Portus Rutupiae*
Chester	*Deva*	St Albans	*Verulamium*
Chesterholm	*Vindolanda*	Silchester	*Calleva Atrebatum*
Chichester	*Noviomagus Regnorum*	Staines	*Pontes*
Cirencester	*Corinium Dobunnorum*	Water Newton	*Durobrivae*
Colchester	*Camulodunum*	Winchester	*Venta Belgarum*
Corbridge	*Coriosopitum?*	Wroxeter	*Viroconium Cornoviorum*
Dorchester (Dorset)	*Durnovaria*	York	*Eboracum*
Exeter	*Isca Dumnoniorum*		

APPENDIX 3: ROMAN ROADS WITH TRADITIONAL NAMES

The table shows the traditional names of the principal Roman roads, along with their Margary numbers (see chapter 4). Origins and destinations are also included, but note that the implied direction of a particular road is entirely arbitrary. The table does not include minor Roman roads that have names but are given three digits by Margary's numbering system, or those with numbers but no name (see Ivan Margary's books, or the Appendix in Davies 2002 for a full list, and more details of routes).

Traditional road name	Margary number	Origin	Destination
Ackling Dyke	4	Old Sarum	Badbury Rings
Akeman Street	16	St Albans	Cirencester
Akeman Street	23	Cambridge	Littleport
Dere Street	8	York	Newstead
Devil's Causeway	84	Corbridge	Berwick
Devil's Highway	4	London	Silchester
Ermin Street	41	Silchester	Gloucester
Ermine Street	2	London	York
Fen Road	25	Upton	Denver
Foss Way	5	Axminster	Lincoln
High Street	74	Penrith	Ambleside
Icknield Street	333	Babraham	Huntstanton
King Street	26	Ailsworth	Ancaster
King Street	70	Sandbach	Warrington
Maiden Way	84	Kirkby Thore	Carvoran
Military Way	86	Hadrian's Wall	Hadrian's Wall
Military Way	90	Antonine Wall	Antonine Wall
Peddars Way	33	Ixworth	Holme
Port Way	4	Silchester	Old Sarum

Traditional road name	Margary number	Origin	Destination
Pye Road	3	Baylham	Caistor
Roman Ridge	28	Doncaster	Tadcaster
Ryknild Street	18	Bourton	Rotherham
Salt Way	58	Six Hills	Grantham
Sarn Helen	69	Tyn y Groes	Llanio
Sarn Helen (East)	62	Llandovery	Llanfair-Clydogan
Stane Street	15	London	Chichester
Stane Street	32	Braughing	Colchester
Stanegate	85	Corbridge	Carlisle
Stone Street	12	Canterbury	Lympne
Stone Street	36	Halesworth	Woodton
The Great Road	3	London	Colchester
via Devana	24	Godmanchester	Colchester
Wade's Causeway	81	Malton	Whitby
Watling Street	1	Dover	Wroxeter
Watling Street (West)	6	Chester	Monmouth
Well Path	77	Crawford	Dalswinton
White Way/Salt Way	55	Cirencester	Hailes

INDEX

Page numbers in italic refer to illustrations